VALENTIJN DHAENENS

BigmoutH / SmallWaR

TWO PLAYS

OBERON BOOKS
LONDON

WWW.OBERONBOOKS.COM

First published in 2014 by Oberon Books Ltd
521 Caledonian Road, London N7 9RH
Tel: +44 (0) 20 7607 3637 / Fax: +44 (0) 20 7607 3629
e-mail: info@oberonbooks.com
www.oberonbooks.com

A catalogue record for this book is available from the British Library.

PB ISBN: 978-1-78319-169-7
E ISBN: 978-1-78319-668-5

Cover image copyright © daily dolores
BigmoutH image on page 12 copyright © Maya Wilsens
SmallWaR image on page 60 copyright © Inge Lauwers

Visit www.oberonbooks.com to read more about all our books and to buy them. You will also find features, author interviews and news of any author events, and you can sign up for e-newsletters so that you're always first to hear about our new releases.

Contents

BigmoutH

The speeches as used in the performance of *BigmoutH* may differ to a greater or lesser extent from the original on which they are based. They have been used as an inspiration and subsequently been abbreviated, mixed, looped, translated, modernized, combined and paraphrased. It is the author's opinion that speeches are principally about manipulating people. He in turn has manipulated the speeches.

Song1 'Lamb of God' – 'Agnus Dei'

1 The Grand Inquisitor 1583

2 Nicola Sacco 1927

3 Socrates 399BC

Song2 'We'll meet again'

4 Goebbels 1943 / Patton 1945

Song3 'Marche Funèbre' – Chopin

5 Pericles 431BC

Song4 Brabançonne

6 His Majesty King Boudewijn 1990

7 Lumumba 1960

Song5&6 / 8 MIX-AMERICANA: '(*I wanna live in*) *America*' – R. Kennedy 1968 – M.L. King 1968 – Malcolm X 1964 – M. ALI 1974 – J.F.K. 1961 – Reagan 1986 – '*Fly me to the moon*' – H.W. Bush 1991

9 Louis Farrakhan 2005

10 Osama Bin Laden 1996

11 Frank Van Hecke 2007

Song7 'Smells like teen spirit' – K. Cobain 1991

12 G.W. Bush 2001 / 2006

13 Ann Coulter 2001

14 G.W. Bush 2002

Song8 'Nature Boy'

SONG 1 *AGNUS DEI*

Agnus dei
Qui tollis peccata mundi
Dona nobis pacem
> Lamb of God,
> you who take away the sins of the world,
> grant us peace.

1 THE GRAND INQUISITOR

Agnus Dei qui vocaris, et Iesus Nazarenus, Messias,
filius patris nescio cuius, propheta, Iudaeus, Christus et
Dominus,
Domine, non sum dignus ut intres sub tectum meum, sed
tantum dic verbo, et sanabitur anima mea,
si tu is es vere

> Lamb of God, Jesus of Nazareth, Messiah, son of…
> prophet, Jew, Christ, Lord,
> I am not worthy to receive you, but…
> only say the word, and I shall be healed.
> If you are the one…

Waarom bent u teruggekomen op aarde?

Ik zal u morgen tot de brandstapel moeten veroordelen.

Voor ketterij.

En de mensen die vandaag uw voeten kussen zullen morgen
op mijn gebaar hout komen brengen.

Om u te verbranden.

De meesten zijn zwak.

U zijn enkel de paar sterken dierbaar.

Ook de zwakken, de verdorvenen heb ik lief.

Zij bewonderen mij
omdat ik de last van hun vrijheid wil dragen
en hen leiden,
in uw naam.

Zij worden wel vrij geboren. Maar niet lang daarna
ontwikkelen zij een behoefte aan gemeenschappelijke

adoratie. En daarom hebben ze goden uitgevonden. Dan konden ze naar elkaar roepen: 'verlaat die goden van u en aanbid die van ons of we doen u dood.'

En geloof mij, zelfs als alle goden al lang van deze wereld verdwenen zijn,
dan nog zullen ze idolen zoeken waar ze voor kunnen buigen en in bewondering staan.

U wilt de ongedwongen liefde van de mens.

Dat hij u vrijwillig volgt.

Dat hij maar zelf beslist tussen goed en kwaad.

Wat een kwelling; al die keuzes, zoveel beslissingen.

Zo heeft u de kudde uiteengedreven.

Ik zal ze weer bijeenvoegen.

ik zal niet ontkennen dat zij zwak zijn,
als kinderen.

En dat er geen zoeter geluk bestaat dan dat van een kind.

Zij zullen naar mij opkijken en zich in angst tegen me aan drukken.

Ze zullen zich over mij verwonderen dat ik die miljoenkoppige kudde kon temmen.

Ze zullen mijn woede vrezen maar op een enkel gebaar ook weer vrolijk en zonder zorgen zijn.

Ik zal hen dwingen te werken maar hen toestaan in hun vrije tijd te zondigen.

En als ik hen vergeef, zullen ze mij liefhebben.

Want ik ben het Lam Gods waarop zij hun zonden kunnen laden.

Mijn rijk kome, mijn wil geschiede,
enkel op aarde.

Maar spreek!

Word u maar kwaad, hoor. Ik wil uw liefde niet.

Omdat ik u zelf niet liefheb.

Spreek!

Niemand meer dan u heeft deze brandstapel verdiend.

Ik heb gesproken.

Why have you come back to earth?

Tomorrow I will have to lead you to the stake for heresy.

And those who kiss your feet today on my demand, will bring wood to burn you.

Most are weak.

You care only for the few strong ones.

The weak and the corrupted. I have love for them also.

They admire me

because I wish to carry the burden of their freedom

and guide them in your name.

They were born free. But it is not long before they develop a need for common adoration.

And that is why they invented the gods. That they may shout to one another:

'Abandon your gods and worship our gods or we shall kill you.'

And believe me, even when all gods have long disappeared from this earth, then still, they will find idols to kneel to and before whom they can stand in awe.

You want a man's spontaneous love? For him to follow you voluntarily?

For him to choose alone between good and evil.

What a torment: all these choices, so many decisions.

And so you split the flock.

I will herd them together again.

I will not deny that they are weak like children.

And there is no sweeter happiness than that of a child.

They will look up to me, and in fear, will huddle close against me.

They will wonder at me; that I tamed a herd of more than a million.

They will live in fear of my anger, but one single gesture will chase their worries away and bring joy back.

I will force them to work, but allow them, in their spare time, to sin

And if I forgive them, they will love me.

For I am the Lamb of God, on whom they can lay their sins

My Kingdom come, my Will be done,

But speak!

Go ahead, get mad! I do not want your love.

Because I myself do not love you.

Speak!

Nobody deserves this stake as much as you do.

I have spoken.

2 SACCO – 1927

I never known, never heard, anything so cruel as this Court.

Seven years of prosecution.

I know my sentence will be between two class, oppress class and rich class.

That is why I here, today in courtbox,

I belong to oppress class. You are oppressor. Yes, sir.

I am no speaker. I know, my speak not good.

You know all, Mister Judge, you know all my life.

And here I am again, after seven years of prosecuting me and poor wife, and now you want me execute? I would like keep life.

I never stolen ever, never kill ever, never spill blood ever.

Everybody knows my two arms knows very well. I no need to kill man to make money.

I with two hands can live, very well live.

I fought, battled against crime, that law and church make good, normal.

MA DAI! I not wish to a dog or to a snake what I…

I believe I suffer, for things I am guilty of.

I suffer because I was radical. I am radical.

I suffer because I was foreigner, I am foreigner.

But I am so sure to be innocent, so sure to be right

if you execute me two times, I reborn two times, I do what I have always done the same. Again and again and again.

3 SOCRATES

Men of Athens,

I honour you and love you,

But I shall obey God rather than you.

You may acquit me or not,
I shall never alter my ways,
Even if I should have to die many times.

If you let me be killed, you will not easily find another like me
who during his life has not sought material gain and bodily
fulfilment.

I have sought to fulfil my soul with the jewels of wisdom, of
patience,
and above all with the love of freedom.

If you wish to rid yourselves of a fellow man in this unjust way,
so be it.

I must only ask of you, when my sons are grown up, to
punish them;
and trouble them, as I have troubled you,
if they seem to care more about riches, than about virtue.

If they pretend to be something while they are really nothing,
then reprove them, as I have reproved you.

And if you do this, both I and my sons will have received
some justice at your hands.

So. That's it.

The hour of departure has arrived, and we go our ways – I
to die, you to live.

Which is better, God only knows.

SONG 2 WE'LL MEET AGAIN

We'll meet again, don't know where, don't know when

But I'm sure we'll meet again some sunny day.

4 GOEBBELS / **PATTON**

Ich weiß nicht, wie viele Millionen Menschen heute Abend meine Zuhörer sind. Ich möchte zu Ihnen allen aus tiefstem Herzen sprechen. Sie wissen wie schwierig es um die Lage des Reiches bestellt ist.

Es ist jetzt nicht der Augenblick, danach zu fragen, wie alles gekommen ist. Nein, Wir müssen handeln, und zwar unverzüglich, schnell und gründlich, so wie es immer gewesen ist.

> I do not know how many millions of people are listening to me tonight.
> I want to speak to all of you from the bottom of my heart.
> You know how grave the situation of our country is.
> Now is not the time to ask how it all happened.
> We must act, immediately, thoroughly, and decisively,
> as it has always been our way.

American men love to fight, traditionally, it's in our blood.

All real American men love the sting and clash of battle.

American men love a winner. American men despise cowards.

That's why Americans have never lost nor will ever lose a war; for the very idea of losing is hateful to a real American man.

Würden wir in diesem Kampf versagen, so verspielten wir damit unsere geschichtliche Mission.

Eine zweitausendjährige Aufbauarbeit ist in Gefahr.

Wir müssen jetzt die Entschlossenheit aufbringen, alles einzusetzen. Der totale Krieg also ist das Gebot der Stunde.

Europas Zukunft hängt von unserem Kampf ab. Wir
stellen unser kostbarstes nationales Blut zur Verfügung.
Und Wer diesen Kampf im übrigen Europa heute noch
nicht versteht, wird uns morgen auf den Knien danken,
dass wir ihn auf uns genommen haben.

If we fail,

we will have failed our historic mission.

What we have built and done over the last two thousand years
is in danger.

We now must be determined to give all we have.

Total war is the demand of the hour. The future of Europe
hangs on our battle.

We are shedding our most valuable national blood in this
battle.

Those who today do not understand our fight,

will thank us tomorrow on bended knees that we courageously
and firmly took on the task.

**You are not all going to die. Only three percent of you
right here will die in a major battle.**

Death must not be feared. Death, in time, comes to all men.

**Every man is scared in his first battle. If he says he's not,
he's a liar.**

**The real hero is the man who fights even though he is
scared.**

**Some men get over their fright in a minute under fire.
For some, it takes an hour. For some, it takes days.**

**But a real American man will never let his fear of death
overpower his honor, his sense of duty, and his innate
manhood.**

Battle is the most magnificent competition in which a

human being can indulge.

It brings out all that is best and it removes all that is base.

We don't want yellow cowards in this Army. They should be killed off like rats.

If not, they will go home after this war and breed more cowards.

The brave men will breed more brave men.

Kill off the Goddamned cowards and we will have a nation of brave men.

Es darf nicht geduldet werden, dass der weitaus größte Teil des Volkes die ganze Bürde des Krieges trägt, und ein kleiner passiver Teil sich an den Lasten und Verantwortung vorbeizudrücken versucht. Wir haben deshalb einige Maßnahmen getroffen.

Eins:

Alle Bars und Nachtlokale werden geschlossen. Ich kann mir nicht vorstellen, dass es heute noch Menschen gibt, die ihre Kriegspflichten voll erfüllen und gleichzeitig bis tief in die Nacht in Amüsierlokalen herumsitzen. Ich muss daraus nur folgern, dass sie es mit ihren Kriegspflichten nicht allzu genau nehmen.

Zwei:

Auch Luxusrestaurants, sind der Schließung verfallen. Es mag sein, dass der eine oder der andere auch während des Krieges noch in der Pflege des Magens eine Hauptaufgabe sieht. Feinschmecker wollen wir wieder nach dem Kriege werden.

Drei:

Meine Damen, was sollen heute nog Modesalons, die keine Waren mehr verkaufen und nur elektrisches Licht, Heizung und menschliche Arbeitskraft verbrauchen, die uns anderswo, vor allem in der Rüstungsproduktion, an allen Ecken und Enden fehlen.

Vier:

Das gleiche gilt für unsere Frisiersalons. Unsere Frauen und Mädchen müssen sich keine Sorgen machen. Sie werden auch ohne 'tralala' unseren siegreich heimkehrenden Soldaten gefallen.

Unsere Feinde behaupten, die Frauen seien nicht in der Lage, den Mann in der Kriegswirtschaft zu ersetzen. In unsere Kriegswirtschaft sind je doch, seit Jahren schon Millionen unsere besten Frauen mit größtem Erfolg tätig. Und niemand verlangt, dass eine Frau, in die schwere Fertigung einer Panzerfabrik arbeiten geht. Es gibt aber eine Unmenge von Fertigungen für die sich eine Frau, auch wenn sie aus bevorzugten Kreisen stammt, ruhig zur Verfügung stellen kann. Vielleicht kann Mama das abendessen nicht immer rechtzeitig fertig haben wenn Papa abends heim kommt. Gemütlich werden wir es uns wieder machen, wenn wir den Sieg in Händen halten.

We cannot tolerate that a majority of the population carries the heaviest burdens of war,

while a few passively try to escape the burdens and responsibilities.

We are therefore compelled to adopt a series of measures.

1. Bars and night clubs will be closed.

I cannot imagine that today, people who are doing their duty for the war effort still have the energy to stay out late into the night in such places.

I can only conclude that they are not taking their responsibilities seriously.

2. Luxury restaurants will be closed.

It can't be that an occasional person thinks that,
even during war, his stomach is the most important thing.
We can become gourmets once again when the war is over.
3. Ladies, what interest in luxury shops that no longer have
anything to sell,
but only use electricity, heating, and human labour
that is lacking everywhere else, particularly in the
armaments industry.
4. This also applies to fashion salons.
Our women and girls must not worry:
without their 'tralala' they will be able to greet our victorious
returning soldiers.
Our enemies maintain that women are not able to replace
men
in the war economy.
In our war economy however, for years,
millions of our best women have been working successfully in
war production.
No one expects a woman to go to work in certain fields of
heavy labour
such as a tank factory.
There are however numerous jobs that do not demand great
physical strength,
and which a woman can do even if she comes from the better
circles.
When papa comes home, mama may not always have a meal
ready.
But we can be comfortable once we have gained victory.

**We want to get the hell over there. The quicker we clean
up this Goddamned German mess, the quicker we can
take a little jaunt against the purple pissing Japs. We're
going to murder those lousy cocksuckers by the bushel-
fucking-basket.**

War is a bloody, killing business.

We've got to spill their blood, before they spill ours.

When shells are hitting all around you and you wipe the dirt off your face and realize that instead it's the blood and guts of what once was your best friend beside you, you'll know what to do!

Ich weiß, dass große Teile unseres Volkes schwere Opfer bringen müssen.

Die Frau wird das am ehesten verstehen, denn sie hat längst erkannt, dass der Krieg, den heute unsere Männer führen, ein Krieg vor allem zum Schutze ihrer Kinder ist.

Zur Steuer der Wahrheit, möchte Ich, zum Schlusz, eine Reihe von Fragen stellen, die Ihr mir nach bestem Wissen und Gewissen beantworten müsst. Insbesondere aber für unsere Feinde, die uns auch heute abend am ihrem Radio zuhören.

Wollt Ihr den totalen Krieg? Wollt Ihr ihn wenn nötig totaler und radikaler, als wir ihn uns heute überhaupt noch vorstellen können?

I know that many of our people are making great sacrifices.

Women surely understand this, because they have already foreseen,

what burdens our men today, is a war to protect her children.

To make the truth plain, however, I want to ask you a series of questions.

I want you to answer them to the best of your knowledge, according to your conscience.

Especially for our enemies, who are massively listening to us on the radio tonight.

Do you really want a total war?

If necessary, do you want a war more total and radical than anything that we can even imagine today?

I don't want to get any messages saying, 'I am holding my position.'

We are not holding a Goddamned thing. Let the Germans do that.

We are advancing constantly and we are not interested in holding onto anything, except the enemy's balls.

Our basic plan is to advance regardless of whether we have to go over, under, or through the enemy.

Seid Ihr bereit, unsere Männer an der Front, die Mittel und Waffen zur Verfügung zu stellen, die sie brauchen, um den Feind den tödlichen Schlag zu versetzen? Billigt Ihr wenn nötig die radikalsten Maßnahmen gegen einen kleinen Kreis, die mitten im Kriege Frieden spielen. Seid Ihr damit einverstanden, dass, wer sich am Krieg vergeht, den Kopf verliert?

Are you ready to provide our fighting fathers and brothers with the men and arms they need to obtain victory?

Do you approve, if necessary, the most radical measures against a small number who pretend there is peace in the middle of war?

Do you agree that those who harm the war effort should lose their right to live?

American men don't surrender. I don't want to hear of any soldier under my command being captured even if he has been hit.

I want men in my command just like the lieutenant, who, with a gun against his chest, jerked off his helmet, and busted the hell out of the Kraut until he was dead.

And, all of that, with a bullet through a lung. Now there was a real American man!

Seid Ihr bereit, mir auf allen meinen Wegen zu folgen und alles zu tun, was nötig ist, um den Krieg zum siegreichen Ende zu führen.

Ihr alle, Kinder unseres Volkes, einem Willensblock

Mit heißem Herzen und kühlem Kopf, seid Ihr bereit.

Wenn Ihr je treu und unverbrüchlich an den Sieg geglaubt habt, dann sicher in dieser Stunde der nationalen Besinnung und der inneren Aufrichtung.

Nun, Volk, steh auf und Sturm, brich los!

Are you ready to follow me down every path, ready to do everything I deem necessary to lead this war to a blessed final victory?

All of you, you are children of our people, forged together in a single block of will-power.

With burning hearts and cool heads you are ready.

If you ever believed firmly and unshakably in victory,

now is the time more than ever, in this hour of national reflection and contemplation.

Now, people rise up and let the storm break loose!

SONG 3
MARCHE FUNEBRE – CHOPIN

5 PERICLES – ATHENS CROWNS HIS SONS

Ces hommes ont combattu et sont morts courageusement.

Convaincus que punir leurs ennemis était plus doux que
n'importe quoi d'autre,
et qu'ils ne pouvaient tomber pour une raison plus noble,
ils ont décidé de se venger au péril de leur propre vie et de
laisser le reste pour ce qu'il était.

Et puis, en un instant, à l'apogée de leur bonheur, ils sont
décédés.

Ainsi eut lieu la fin de ces hommes.

Ils ont librement donné leurs vies
comme le plus beau sacrifice qu'ils pouvaient faire à leur patrie

Leur gloire survivra et sera louée.

Pour cette raison je ne témoigne pas de ma compassion aux
parents des morts ici présents.

Je voudrais plutôt les consoler.

Je sais à quel point il est difficile de se sentir réconforté, car
le bonheur des autres vous rappelle trop souvent cette joie
qui avant allégeait vos cœurs.

Certains d'entre vous sont en âge d'espérer attendre d'autres
enfants,
ceux-là pourront sans doute mieux supporter leur chagrin.

Les enfants qui vont naître feront oublier ceux qui sont
morts maintenant.

A ceux qui ne sont plus dans la fleur de leur vie, je dis:

Soyez satisfait d'avoir été heureux pendant la plus grande
partie de votre vie,

n'oubliez pas que vous n'allez plus vivre longtemps dans la tristesse
et soyez soulagé par la gloire de ceux qui ne sont plus là.

Car seulement l'amour de l'honneur reste éternellement jeune,
et pas les richesses comme certains le prétendent,
c'est l'honneur qui est la joie de l'homme lorsqu'il est vieux et inutile.

J'ai utillisé les mots qui me semblaient adéquats.

Les morts ont été inhumés honorablement.

La ville couronne ses fils, de ce prix,
comme d'une couronne de laurier après les combats qu'ils ont menés.

Et à présent, alors que vous avez pleuré, comme il convient, chacun pour son propre mort,
vous pouvez y aller.

> These men fought and died with courage.
>
> Deeming that the punishment of their enemies was sweeter than any of these things,·
>
> and that they could fall in no nobler cause,
>
> they determined at the hazard of their lives to be honorably avenged, and to leave the rest.
>
> These men they ran away from the word 'dishonor', but on the battlefield their feet stood fast,
>
> and in an instant, at the height of their fortune, they passed away.
>
> Such was the end of these men.
>
> They freely gave their lives to their nation
>
> as the fairest offering which they could present at her feast.
>
> Their glory will live on and be praised.
>
> This is why I do not now pity the parents of the dead who stand here;
>
> I would rather comfort them.

I know how hard it is to make you feel this, when the good fortune of others

will too often remind you of the gladness which once lightened your hearts.

Some of you are of an age at which they may hope to have other children,

and they ought to bear their sorrow better;

the children they will bear will make them forget those we've lost today.

To those of you who have passed their prime, I say:

'Congratulate yourselves that you have been happy during the greater part of your days;

remember that your life of sorrow will not last long,

and be comforted by the glory of those who are gone.

For the love of honor alone is ever young,

and not riches, as some say,

but honor is the delight of men when they are old and useless.

I have paid the required tribute, making use of such fitting words as I had.

The dead have been buried honorably.

The city crowns her sons,

living and dead, with this solid prize, like a garland, after a struggle like theirs.

And now, when you have duly lamented,

every one his own dead,

you may depart.

SONG 4

BRABANCONNE (Belgian National Anthem) the Hendrix-way.

But woe to you if, wilfully,
Pursuing dreadful plans,
You turn on us
The bloody cannon's fire!

6 BOUDEWIJN – ABORTUS

'Het duurt twintig jaar of meer om een man te maken; het
duurt slechts twintig seconden om een man te breken.'

'It takes twenty years and more to make a man,
but only twenty seconds to break him.'

Waarde landgenoten,

Op 29 maart heeft het parlement een wet goedgekeurd die
abortus liberaliseert. Op 6 november is de wet aanvaard
door de senaat. Volgens de Belgische Grondwet kan geen
enkele wet die aldus door beide Kamers is goedgekeurd
afgekondigd worden zonder te zijn voorzien van de
handtekening van mijzelf, de koning.

Eerbiediging van het leven van het te geboren worden kind
is voor mij en Fabiola een heilig en universeel beginsel.
«Het kind, heeft vanwege zijn gebrek aan lichamelijke
en verstandelijke rijpheid, behoefte aan bijzondere
bescherming, bijzondere zorg, met name aan adequate
juridische bescherming zowel voor als na de geboorte». «Dit
wetsontwerp stelt mij voor een groot gewetensprobleem...
ik ben van oordeel dat ik onvermijdelijk een zekere
medeverantwoordelijkheid voor mijn rekening zou nemen.
Dat kan ik niet doen».

God vraagt niet dat wij technisch deskundig zijn op de
meest uiteenlopende gebieden, maar dat wij, geleid door
zijn Geest, de mensen beminnen met zijn Liefde, hen
bekijken met zijn ogen, naar hen luisteren met zijn oren,
tegen hen spreken met zijn woorden. Het goede te doen.
Dat verlangen wij, Fabiola en ik, met heel onze ziel.
de abortuswet die door het Belgisch parlement is
goedgekeurd is in tegenspraak met het goede dat wordt

uitgedrukt in de wet van God. «Onder de misdrijven die de mens tegen
oor die bijzonder zwaarwegend en verwerpelijk wordt.

Om deze redenen bevind ik mij in de feitelijke onmogelijkheid dit land te regeren en zie ik mij genoodzaakt af te treden als Koning der Belgen.

Om mijn motivatie kracht bij te zetten, sluit ik graag af met de woorden van de heilige Teresia van Lisieux:

'O, mijn God, om U te beminnen op aarde, heb ik niets dan vandaag'

Dear fellow citizens,

On March 29, Parliament approved a law decriminalizing abortion.

On November 6, the law was accepted by the Senate.

According to the Belgian Constitution no law approved by both houses can be enacted without first being signed by myself, the King.

Respect for the life of the unborn child is, for me and Fabiola, a sacred and universal principle.

The child because of his lack of physical and intellectual maturity, needs special protection, special care, especially legal protection before, as well as after birth.

This proposed law raises a great problem of conscience for me…

I would inevitably take on a certain degree of co-responsibility. That I cannot do.

God does not ask us to be technically expert in the most divergent fields, but guided by his Spirit, that we love people with his Love,

that we see them with His eyes, that we listen with His ears, that we speak with His words.

To accomplish good deeds.

This is what we desire, Fabiola and me, with all our hearts

The Abortion Act which was approved by Parliament
is in opposition to good as expressed in the law of God.
Among all the crimes which can be committed against life,
procured abortion has characteristics
making it particularly burdensome to carry and condemnable.
For these reasons I find myself unable de facto to rule the country
and this forces me to abdicate as King of the Belgians.
To strengthen my motivation, I will conclude with words of
Saint Therese of Lisieux:
'Oh my God, to love You on earth, I have nothing but today'

7 PATRICE LUMUMBA – CONGO INDEPENDENCE

Sa Majesté le roi Baudouin, élus, citoyens,

Au nom du gouvernement congolais, je vous salue,
Combattants de l'indépendance aujourd'hui victorieux.

Et meme, si elle est proclamée aujourd'hui dans l'entente
avec la Belgique.

Nul Congolais digne de ce nom ne pourra jamais oublier
cependant que c'est par la lutte
qu'elle a été conquise.

Une lutte dans laquelle nous n'avons ménagé ni nos forces,
ni nos souffrances, ni notre sang.

Une lutte indispensable pour mettre fin à l'humiliant
esclavage.

80 ans de régime colonialiste.

Nous avons connu le travail harassant exigé en échange de
salaires qui ne nous permettaient ni de manger à notre faim,
ni de nous loger décemment, ni d'élever nos enfants comme
des êtres chers.

Nous avons connus les insultes, parce que nous étions des nègres.

Nous avons connu nos terres spoliées au nom de textes
prétendument légaux.

Et qui oubliera, enfin, les fusillades où périrent tant de nos frères,
les cachots où furent brutalement jetés ceux qui ne
voulaient plus se soumettre au régime d'une justice
d'oppression et d'exploitation!

Tout cela nous avons supporté.

Mais nous, la voix de vos élus,
nous vous affirmons aujourd'hui très fort que tout cela est
définitivement terminé.

Notre pays est à présent dans les mains de ses propres
enfants.

Nous allons montrer au monde ce que peut faire l'homme
noir lorsqu'il travaille dans la liberté.

Nous allons faire du Congo le centre de rayonnement de
l'Afrique toute entière.

Nous n'allons pas régner dans la paix des canons et des baïonnettes
mais grâce à la paix du cœur et de la volonté.

Et sachez, mes chers concitoyens,
que notre nouveau Congo héberge une immense richesse en
matières premières.

Soyez rassurés, il y en aura enfin assez pour tout le monde.

Et je voudrais ajouter ceci encore:

l'indépendance du Congo marque un pas décisif vers la
libération de tout le continent africain.

Sire, excellences, mesdames, messieurs, mes chers
concitoyens,
mes frères de race, mes frères de lutte,
c'est ce que je voulais vous dire au nom du gouvernement
en ce beau jour de totale indépendance.

Vive l'indépendance et l'unité africaine!

Vive le Congo indépendant et souverain!

KRK KRK, BANG! Aaaaaaa...

His majesty King Bauduoin, Elected officials, Citizens,

In the name of the Congolese Government I greet you
Victorious fighters for a victorious independence.

And even as it is celebrated today with Belgium,

no Congolese worthy of the name will ever be able to forget
that is was by fighting

that it has been won.

A fight in which we were spared neither privation nor
suffering, and for which we gave our blood.

A fight to put an end to the humiliating slavery.

Eighty years of a colonial regime:

We have known harassing work, exacted in exchange for
salaries which did not permit us to eat enough to drive away
hunger, or to house ourselves decently, or to raise our children
as creatures dear to us.

We have known insults, blows because we are Negroes.

We have seen our lands seized in the name of allegedly legal laws.

And who will ever forget the massacres where so many of our
brothers perished,

the cells into which those who refused to submit

to a regime of oppression and exploitation were thrown?

All that, my brothers, we have endured.

But we, the voice of your elected representatives,

we tell you very loud, all that is henceforth ended.

Our country is now in the hands of its own children.

We are going to show the world what the black man can do
when he works in freedom.

We are going to make of the Congo the centre of the sun's
radiance for all of Africa.

We are going to rule not by the peace of guns and bayonets
but by a peace of the heart and the will.

And know this, my fellow citizens:

our new Congo bears an immense wealth in raw materials.

Be reassured, there will finally be enough for everyone.

And there's more:

Congo's independence marks a decisive step towards the liberation of the entire African continent

Sire, Excellencies, Ladies, and Gentleman, my dear fellow countrymen,

my brothers of race, my brothers of struggle,

this is what I wanted to tell you on this magnificent day of our complete independence.

Long live independence and African unity!

Long live the independent and sovereign Congo!

SONG5
AMERICA

I wanna live in America

okay by me in America

everything's free in America

for a small fee in America.

8 MIX-AMERICANA (R. Kennedy 1968 – M.L. King 1968 – Malcolm X 1964 – M. ALI 1974 – J.F.K. 1961 – Reagan 1986 – H.W. Bush 1991)

FREE AT LAST, FREE AT LAST, THANK GOD ALMIGHTY, WE ARE FREE AT LAST.

I had prepared another speech for this evening. But I have some very sad news for all of you,

Martin Luther King was shot and killed tonight in Memphis, Tennessee.

In these difficult times, it might be a good idea to ask ourselves what kind of a nation we actually are? I WANNA LIVE...

Like anybody, I would like to live a long life.

Longevity has its place.

But it doesn't matter with me now.

Because I've been to the mountaintop. And I've seen the promised land.

I may not get there with you. But we, as a people, will get to the promised land. KRK KRK BANG

My land, sweet land of liberty, land where my fathers died, land of the pilgrim's pride, from every moutainside let it ring:

Free at last! Free at last! Thank God Almighty, we are free at last! I WANNA LIVE...

I'M SO MEAN I MAKE MEDICINE SICK

We are not American. We are African. Africans who happen to be in America.

We are Africans who were kidnapped and brought to America.

If you are interested in freedom, you will have to fight for that freedom.

I'm young, I'm handsome, I'm pretty, I'm fast.

I can't possibly be beaten.

I have wrestled with an alligator, have wrestled with a whale.

Only yesterday, I murdered a rock, injured a stone, hospitalized a brick. I WANNA LIVE...

I DID NOT HAVE SEXUAL RELATIONS WITH THAT WOMAN

HAPPY BIRTHDAY MR PRESIDENT

Today, man holds in his mortal hands

the power to abolish all forms of human poverty and all forms of human life.

KRK KRK BANG I WANNA LIVE...

I love my little girls more than anything.
I would rather see them die now; still believing in God,
than have them grow up under communism and one day die
no longer believing in God.

SONG6 FLY ME TO THE MOON

Fly me to the moon and let me play among the stars, let me see what spring is like on Jupiter and Mars.

Nancy and I want to say something to the schoolchildren who were watching the explosion of the shuttle's take-off, today on television. I know it's hard to understand, but sometimes painful things like this happen. It's all part of the process of exploration and discovery. The Challenger crew was pulling us into the future, and we'll continue to follow them. They were and stay pioneers, and it was pioneers that made this country. I WANNA LIVE...

WE HAVE NOTHING TO FEAR BUT FEAR ITSELF. MAY GOD BLESS AMERICA.

I'm sure that many of you saw on the television the unforgettable scene of four terrified Iraqi soldiers surrendering.

They emerged from their bunker; broken, tears streaming from their eyes, fearing the worst.

And then there was an American soldier. He said:

'It's okay. You're all right now. Have no fear. It's all over.

You're good now, you're good now.'

9 LOUIS FARRAKHAN – NATION OF ISLAM

America is no good at all. If you make a promise that you don't keep, you're no good. What are you? You are a liar. Did they fulfill their promise to the native Americans? I don't think so.

Didn't President Johnson promise land to the freed slaves after using them for turning the American industry into the strongest of the world with the sweat of our free labour? Did they fulfill it? I don't think so.

Equal education for all? Fifty years on, and we are still in segregated schools.

The right to vote? You got it. But the minute they gave it to you they were finding ways to take it back from you. Suddenly, we were required to register one full year before the elections. The call up letters, however, were abolished.

Have you moved these last months? No vote. Do you live in a trailer? No vote. Ever committed a crime? Never vote. In the state of Florida alone, 31 percent of all black men have already lost their right to vote forever.

And they won't stop. A new law allows them to deprive millions of legal workers of their right to vote because they were not born on U.S. territory.

And now the black nation is said to be ready to enter into an agreement with these people that lied to us, deceived us, murdered us and robbed us.

Dear Chairman, If you lack the testicular fortitude to say what needs to be said then sit down and stop trying to say you are speaking for our people and the herd of the poor. So don't look at him, look to God, look to yourself, break your agreement with hell, with death. Make an agreement with black America, implement a road map that frees us of the white oppressor.

For those at the top there's only way, and it goes straight to hell.

And if I do have any power, I intend to push them into hell as fast as I can.

We are a full nation now. And we have to stop thinking like negroes, like slaves.

We are free men and women now,
who don't wanna live on a plantation no more.

I gotta go now. Love you all.

10 OSAMA BIN LADEN – 1996

I would like to take this opportunity, to give the Western world
and in particular the American people,
an understanding of the hatred that fills my heart and the
heart of one billion Muslims and that we carry against the
United States of America and its presidents, in this moment
Mr. Bill Clinton.

The events that affected my soul in a direct way started in 1982
when America permitted the Israelis to invade Lebanon
and the American Sixth Fleet helped them.

This bombardment began
I couldn't forget those moving scenes,
blood and severed limbs, children sprawled everywhere.
Houses destroyed along with their occupants.
Thousands of rockets raining down on our homes without mercy.

The situation was like a crocodile meeting a helpless child,
powerless except for his screams.

Does the crocodile understand a conversation that doesn't
include a weapon?

And the whole world saw and heard but it didn't respond.

In those difficult moments many hard-to-describe ideas
bubbled in my soul,
but in the end gave birth to a strong resolve to punish the
oppressors.

We declared jihad against the US government,
because we think it's unjust, criminal and tyrannical.

Because we believe its support to the Israeli occupier

is directly responsible for those who were killed in Palestine, Lebanon and Iraq.

And you, the American people are not exonerated from responsibility,
because you chose this government despite your knowledge of its crimes
in Palestine, Lebanon, Iraq and in other places in the world.

The collapse of the Soviet Union made the US arrogant. It has started to look at itself as a Master of this world and established what it calls a new world order.

Since that day, it wants to occupy our countries, steal our resources,
and impose their way of life as the only possible way.

Those who refuse to do so, they call terrorists.

The Palestinian children that throw stones against the Israeli occupier,
they call terrorists whereas they don't condemn the Israeli pilots who bombed the United Nations building in Lebanon while full of children and women.

While condemning any Muslim who calls for his right,
they receive the highest IRA official at the White House as a political leader.

Neither do the US consider it a terrorist act to throw atomic bombs
at nations thousands of miles away,
knowing all too well that those bombs will make hundreds of thousands of innocent civilian victims.

In short, we consider the US to be the leader of terrorism

and crime in the world.

Therefore, it is not difficult for us, Muslims, to give a meaning to our duty to Allah, *Alhamdulilah*.

And we ask Allah to reward the martyrs that killed, in Riyad and Khobar,
the American occupiers.

Over the past seven years, several attempts to eliminate me took place and have invariably failed.

This is proof that America is weaker and less effective than the image it likes to give of itself.

Our life is in the hands of Allah only.

I want to fight on behalf of Allah and be killed.

I'll do it again and be killed
and do it again and once again be killed.

We love death as much as you love life.

That is why always we will inevitably win in the end.

Because we are prepared for the greatest sacrifice.
Wait and see.

11 FRANK VANHECKE IN AMERICA – 2007

Yes, yes. If I may just have your attention for a few minutes here in, euh… Well, euh, mostly here. Now, before I introduce myself I want to thank Mr Pat Buchanan for inviting me here in the United States of America. I am very happy to be here. Thank you very much Mr. Pat, euh, Buchanan. Now, before I start off, I wanna apologize a little bit for my poor speaking of your language. Well, euh… It's your language, not my language. But I have a very good translator and she has translated my speech from my language into your language. So I'm quite sure you will all understand me very clear and, euh, brightly.

My name is Frank Vanhecke.
I am a member of the European Parliament.
In my country, Belgium, I am currently standing trial as a criminal because I am member of the Vlaams Belang, the largest political party in the country.

I was brought before the court because of a statement I made in an interview with *The Jewish Week*, that's a Jewish magazine. When the journalist asked me whether 'Jews should vote for a party that cultivates xenophobia' I answered: 'If it absolutely must be a "phobia," let it be "Islamophobia."'

Now, to say 'islamophobia' in Belgium is criminal.

But in real; The Belgian authorities want to rob us of our finances. That's why they brought us to court.

We are sure that we will be convicted because it is a political trial, pushed by a regime that considers it a crime to tell the truth.

Belgium is a country consisting of two nations, Dutch-speaking Flemings in the north and French-speaking Walloons in the south.

My party strives for the independence of Flanders. So without the Walloons.

Most immigrants in Belgium are Muslims. People who come purely for the purpose of claiming benefits.
These people sympathize with the parties of the Left. And now they can also vote. We fear that in the coming decades the impact of the immigrant vote will move European politics dramatically to the left. That will also affect American-European relations.

Our voters want to live in Europe, not in Eurabia.

Europe is gradually becoming a totalitarian society.
We think, you Americans should realize this.

Every day we see that Eurabia is not a myth. It is becoming reality before our own eyes.

Thousands of third-world Muslims, have immigrated to Europe. Europe is about to be taken over, without a fight, by aliens who are hostile to Western civilization. The number of Muslims is increasing rapidly also because of the high birthrates. The immigrant population is very young, the European population is aging. Our children are about to become a minority in the land of their ancestors. We are becoming foreigners in our own land.

Bernard Lewis, a professor at the University of Princeton has predicted – quote: 'Europe will be a part of the Arab West, of the Maghreb. Migration and demographics point in this direction. Europeans marry late and have no or few children. But there is also a high rate of immigration: Turks in Germany, Arabs in France and Pakistanis in England. They marry young and have many children. Current trends indicate that Europe's population will include a Muslim majority by the end of the 21st century at the latest.' – unquote.

Just a few decades ago the Muslim population in Europe was hundred thousand. Now 23 million Muslims live in Europe.

In Brussels, the capital of Europe, the name most frequently given to newborn boys is Mohammed.

Islam is like a koekoek (the bird) who lays its egg in the European nest, but once the egg is ready it treats its host with utter hostility.

In many European cities riots involving Muslim youths have become a routine.

In Paris the muslims burned almost 9,000 cars and buses as well as buildings. Many of Europe's cities contain zones where the state or the police have lost all authority.

They are a threat to our national security.

Time is running out for Europe. Europe is at war. At war with a gang of religious fanatics who are out to destroy our values, our democracy, our society.

We are fighting for survival, and for the survival of our children. We are living on a dying continent, but we are not dead yet. The Vlaams Belang, is fighting back.

Help us survive. Tell America what is happening to us. If you do not remain silent, the Belgian authorities will never be able to silence us.

Thank you very much for your attention. And thank you again Mr Pat Buchanan, for heaving us here, in this beautiful, room.

And I hope you enjoy your stay

No, no. I'm staying here.

SONG7 SMELLS LIKE TEEN SPIRIT – K. COBAIN

I found it hard	It's hard to find
Oh well, whatever,	NEVERMIND

12 BUSH 9/11 – **KATRINA**

Good evening.
Today, our fellow citizens, our way of life, our very freedom
came under attack in a series of deliberate and deadly
terrorist acts.
The victims were in airplanes, or in their offices;
secretaries, businessmen and women, military and federal
workers; moms and dads, friends and neighbors.
Thousands of lives were suddenly ended by evil itself.

**I am speaking to you from the city of New Orleans –
nearly empty,
still partly under water, and waiting for life and hope to return.
Millions of lives were changed in a day by a cruel and
wasteful storm.**

The pictures of airplanes flying into buildings, have filled us
with disbelief, terrible sadness, and a quiet, unyielding anger.
These acts of mass murder were intended to frighten our
way of living.
But they have failed.
Terrorist attacks can shake the foundations of our buildings,
but never the foundation of America.

**I have seen fellow citizens left uprooted, in search
for loved ones, and grieving for the dead, looking for
meaning in a tragedy that seems so blind and random.**

**Vulnerable people left at the mercy of criminals
and the bodies of the dead lying uncovered and
untended in the street.**

Why America?

Because we're the brightest beacon for freedom and opportunity in the world.

What did they forget?

The world's most powerful and mighty military, and we're prepared.

It won't take long to find those responsible for these evil acts and bring them to justice.

And make no mistake about it; We will make no distinction between the terrorists and those who harbor them.

Luckily we have people like Steve Scott of the Biloxi Fire Department, in search for survivors. Steve told me this:

'I lost my house and I lost my cars,
but I still got my family...
and more important I still got my spirit.'

It is that same spirit we need today:
a core of strength that survives all hurt.
A faith in God no storm can take away.
Psalm 23: 'Even though I walk through the valley of the
shadow of death, I fear no evil, for You are with me.'

13 ANN COULTER

Not all Muslims may be terrorists,
but all terrorists are Muslims –
at least all terrorists capable of leaving with two airplanes
7,000 people dead in under two hours.
But the FBI refuses to screen people on the basis of race or
origin.
Doing so, the FBI acknowledged that, last week, 7000
Americans were slaughtered on the altar of political
correctness.
Airports scrupulously apply the same laughably ineffective
airport harassment to Suzy Chapstick as to Muslim
hijackers.
It is preposterous to assume every passenger is a potential
crazed homicidal maniac.
We know who the homicidal maniacs are.
They are the ones cheering and dancing right now.
We should invade their countries,
kill their leaders and convert their inhabitants to
Christianity.
We weren't punctilious about locating and punishing only
Hitler.
We carpet-bombed all of Germany.
We killed civilians.
That's war. And this is war.

14 G.W. BUSH – STATE OF THE UNION 2002

For many Americans, these four months have brought sorrow, and pain that will never completely go away.

I know a retired firefighter who travels 200 miles a day to Ground Zero, to feel closer to his two sons who died there.

At a memorial in New York, a little boy left his football with a note:

'Dear Daddy, please take this to heaven.
I don't want to play football until I can play with you again some day'.

Little Tom, I assure you that this country, your country will never forget the debt we owe to your daddy.

Fortunately, there is still your mommy...
Unless of course you have two papas, which is also apparently possible now...
But then you probably wouldn't want to play football, but, do some basketball
or synchronized swimming
or softball...
But, uh, well, there's still your mommy.
It won't be easy for her now, alone in her small house.
Maybe you can tell her to give me a call...
Maybe she sometimes feels the need to cry on a strong shoulder.
We can get that done. Could even do it the oval office...
Laughing and joking apart...

SONG8
NATURE BOY – NAT KING COLE

The greatest thing you'll ever learn

Is just to love and be loved in return.

THE END

SmallWaR

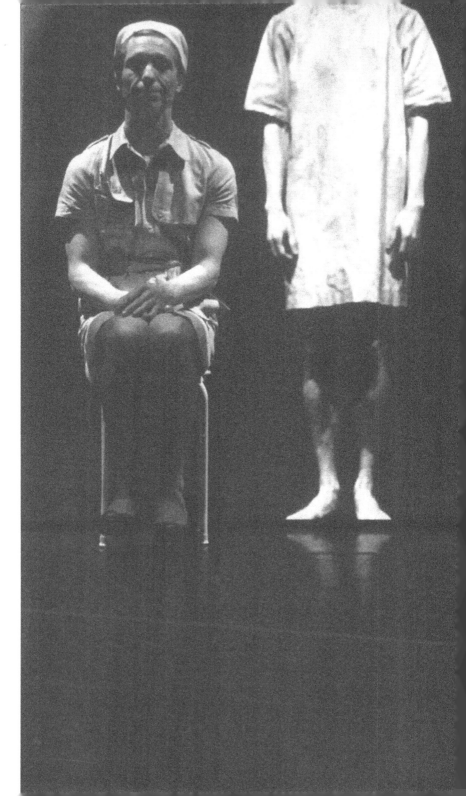

— 41 TRAUMA BEATS —

1 BIGMOUTHS
2 *SONG* NATURE BOY
3 CUT AWAY
4 BODY PARTS
5 PROLONGING
6 FROM SCRATCH
7 HUT
8 *SONG* SMILE
9 BAD LUCK
10 *SONG* SMILE *part2*
11 *TELEPHONE* SHOULD GO HOME
12 WITHOUT ASKING
13 CLEAN SHEETS
14 THE THING
15 THE GAP
16 AGNUS DEI
17 SILVER CROSS
18 GIVE LIFE
19 THE RING
20 *TELEPHONE* SWEETHEART
21 GONE
22 WILLINGLY
23 THE VOW
24 NOT MADE OF STONE
25 *SONG* ARE YOU LONESOME TONIGHT
26 BEAN
27 THE MIRACLE
28 TELEPHONE HARVEST MOON
29 NOT FOR ME
30 THE FASCINATION
31 THE FULL UNIFORM
32 TELEPHONE DEMOCRACY
33 THE BEAST
34 ATILLA THE HUN
35 *SONG* RIDERS ON THE STORM
36 THE ETERNAL SHORE
37 THE SYNDROME
38 A DREAM
39 TELEPHONE CAN'T TALK
40 *SONG* SILENT NIGHT
41 NOT EVEN GOD

---

1 BIGMOUTHS

Voiceover

Someone tapped you on the shoulder and said: 'Come along, we're going to war'. So you went. You go out to fight for liberty. A peculiar word. Maybe you'll sacrifice your life for liberty. That is what men always have done. If they're not fighting for liberty, they fight for independence, democracy, honour or their native land. Men have always been killed for this freedom. And if we win the war, we'll get that freedom. If you die, you sacrifice your life for something that is worth more to you than your life: this freedom.

There are always going to be bigmouths who are willing to sacrifice somebody else's life. They're plenty loud and talk well. That's their job. You can find them in churches and schools, in newspapers and congresses, on raised platforms or in the crowd. They speak of men who died gloriously, who shall not have died in vain. The noble dead who gave their lives so that we could live.

When they watch their blood pumping out into the mud. When the gas hits their lungs and burns them away. When, in the final phase, they are lying crazed and look death straight in the face. Do they think of democracy and freedom and honour. Maybe they realize that life is indivisible and everything. Not a happy, honourable or free life. I couldn't care less. When I'm dead, I simply want life back. To be something that moves over the ground and isn't dead. Nobody dies for something.

2 *SONG* **NATURE BOY**

There was a boy

A very strange, enchanted boy…

3 CUT AWAY

Nurse

I hate cannons.

The ceaseless thunder of cannons.

And then: ambulances

The endless procession of ambulances.

They throw off the broken soldiers, here.

Then a quick return.

To fetch more broken soldiers.

They will arrive later on.

First: the waiting room.

On the floor, against the wall, on the window-sill.
Everywhere.

Sometimes they scream. Sometimes they stay mute.

I cut away the clothes around their wounds.

They drop on the floor, soaked mostly, mud or blood.

Then we carry the body to the operating theatre.

Boiling hot in there.

One pulls away a blanket.

One determines this is a man.

One assesses the scale of the wounds.

One rinses out the dried-up blood from the edges of the
wound.

One discusses, evaluates, speculates and proceeds.

I'm not allowed to do anything.

I have to wait... until they call for me.

//

In 15% of the cases a wounded Englishman will not survive this operation. A German in 17% of the cases. A Frenchman in 25% of the cases. And a Russian at the Eastern Front has only 1 chance in 2 to overcome his injuries.

//

Belgians, I don't know, time will tell.

4 BODY PARTS

Voiceover

They pull away a blanket.

They assess the scale of my wounds.

They discuss the different parts of my body

In terms I don't understand.

But I listen.

I can only move my tongue.

I try to wet my lips with my tongue.

5 PROLONGING

Nurse

Often, they tend to prolong his suffering three more weeks.
That's all.

They never dwell on the fact that this life-saving might
not be indicated in the normal world. These wretches have
already done their utmost after all. And defended our most
precious values.

6 FROM SCRATCH

Voiceover

Then they dive into the gaping mouth of my wounds.
Those helpless stinking holes.

Of course they are eager to make groundbreaking
discoveries. On those who would die as a result of their
wounds they try absolutely everything. Bones, muscles,
blood vessels, tendons. They start from scratch. As if they
have no previous knowledge, hoping the body will divulge
a new secret? A secret which in peacetime would have been
overlooked.

7 HUT

Nurse

Then they call for me.
I disinfect and bandage what remains or has been stitched.

I lift the front of the stretcher, push open the door with a knee.

Then on to hut 1 for the gravely wounded and dying.

Hut 2: amputations.

3: head injuries. And so on.

Sometimes I get to choose.

Then: lifting the unconscious body into a bed.

One and two and…

And there he lies, dazed and exhausted.

The subject of our interest.

8 *SONG* SMILE

Smile though your heart is aching,

smile even though it's breaking…

9 BAD LUCK

Voiceover

A hand on my chest.

My face, there's something wrong with my face.

Why don't they turn the lights on?

It's dark in here. Dark and still.

I can feel the blood pumping through my veins.

But I can't hear the pulse in my ear.

If you can't hear your own pulse, you're probably deaf.

Am I deaf?

Deaf?

I can feel the sweat pouring out of my skin.

We hear a telephone ringing.

Why is no one answering that phone.

Telephones in the middle of the night are bad luck.

Better not pick up.

It's not going to ring all night, is it?

10 *SONG* SMILE *part2*

You'll find that life is still worthwhile

If you just smile.

11 *TELEPHONE* SHOULD GO HOME

Soldier 1

Hello?

Yes, yes, Mother, I'll come home shortly.

It's tricky, I'm kind of busy here.

It's over, is it? Calm down, Mum. Calm down.

I'll ask.

My father has just passed away. I should go home, I guess.

That's probably not an option, is it?

Nurse shakes her head apologetically.

12 WITHOUT ASKING

Voiceover

Calm down.

They've cut off my arm. They've severed it right off the shoulder. Without asking. I need my arm. How am I going to work now? They didn't think of that. They should've asked first. But no, they just do their own thing.

13 CLEAN SHEETS

Nurse

Before dawn many will follow.

They are now in a place full of passion and struggle,

holding back the enemy.

Without them we would all be swept away.

Now in the prime of their lives

Soon: filthy dying men

in clean beds, under clean sheets.

14 THE THING

Soldier 1

Here lies your brother. Here lies your best friend. Here you lie. Breathing, thinking, helpless but alive. Here lies your future, your wild romantic dreams. Here lies the thing your leaders have made out of him.

15 THE GAP

Nurse

Life is clean.

And death is clean.

The gap in between:

that's a different kettle of fish.

Filthy dregs fill the bottom of most souls.

War is not always a cleansing process

that purifies men and nations

as some claim.

16 AGNUS DEI

Soldier1

Lamb of God, you who take away the sins of the world,

grant us peace.

Set me high on your altars and call on God to look down

upon his murderous little children, his dearly beloved

children.

17 SILVER CROSS

Nurse

The dying are

often decorated just before they pass away

for services rendered.

Some even get the Silver Cross for courage and excellence.

When I feel the end is coming.

After a while, you know, when it's almost over,

I hang his medal at the foot of his bed.

So he can look at it.

Small consolation, I know.

Then I have to find someone to administer the last rites.

I'm not allowed to do that.

18 GIVE LIFE

Soldier 1 playing priest

Repeat after me.

Say it: 'God, I willingly give you my life for my country.'

Last sentence starts looping till BEAT 22.

19 THE RING

Voiceover

Fixing up an arm is probably too expensive. Let's cut it off. Do it. He's bedridden and can't speak anyway. I had a ring on my finger. Where is it now? A ring my sweetheart gave me. Is it lying somewhere? Or still on the dead arm? Where's my arm gone? Buried? In formalin? In the rubbish bin? I really want that ring. It matters to me. It was a gift from my sweetheart and I promised never to take it off.

20 *TELEPHONE* SWEETHEART

Soldier 2 – *Nurse playing Sweety*

Hello Sweety? That ring doesn't fit my finger anymore.

What finger?

My ring finger, of course!

I got that ring from my mother, silly. It only fits your little finger.

Oh yes, of course.

My father said you can spend the night with me.

Really?

Just because you are going to be away a long time?

Exciting.

What?

Spending the night together.

Have you ever been with anyone before?

Not with anyone I loved.

I'm glad.

What about you?

You don't ask a lady these things. Oh please, don't go. I'm so scared. Can't you run away?

When you're drafted you have to go.

They'll kill you.

Maybe. But I don't think so.

Lots of people get killed who didn't think they would.

Lots of people come back. I need to do something.

We'll discuss it later. Hurry up, will you? I want your arms around me.

I'll be right there. Just need to finish something here.

21 GONE

Voiceover
I have no arms, Sweety.
My arms are gone.
Both of them, gone.
They've cut them off.

22 WILLINGLY

Soldier 1 playing Priest
Oh yes, yes, my Lord, yes.
I willingly give you my life for my country.
Willingly! Willingly! Oh yes, yes.

Soldier 2 playing another Priest
Per istam sanctam unctionem et suam piissimam
misericordiam adiuvet
te Dominus gratia Spiritus Sancti,
ut a peccatis liberatum te salvet
atque propitius allevet.

Nurse translates
Through this holy anointing
may the Lord in his love and mercy help you
with the grace of the Holy Spirit.
May the Lord who frees you from sin
save you and raise you up.

23 THE VOW

Nurse

I have decided to choose the most important profession in the world. I can't set myself a higher goal. I am here to prove to myself that I can achieve that goal. The meaning of life and death will become clear to me here. I have to forget all I have experienced, seen and understood so far. From this moment on I no longer have a free will. I will isolate myself from normal society, break any links with my community and, to speed up this adaptation, I will stop myself from writing any letters or making any phone calls. I commit myself to a higher goal and rob myself of all certainties and dignity. // What happens here, will change me forever.

Soldier 2

I will not put the holy arms to shame, nor shall I abandon my fellow soldier // wherever I may find myself in the line of battle. I will defend what is most blessed and sacred and leave a bigger and stronger homeland to my offspring, not a smaller one. Whatever it takes. I will always and immediately obey those who assert their authority wisely, all existing laws and what laws may come into force in the future.

24 NOT MADE OF STONE

Soldier 1

Reading letter like a child who's learning to read.

It has been more than two years since you were home.
A woman also has certain needs.

Since you can't join me here, I have to seek salvation elsewhere.

I mean it. I've never been more serious. I don't care what you make of it.

You can't expect me to just throw away my youth.

I'm not made of stone. I have certain needs. And my patience has run out.

I really feel for you. I will always love you.

The children send their love.

25 *SONG* ARE YOU LONESOME TONIGHT

Nurse
And while I'm so lonely
I'm writing you only
To see if you care for me still…

26 BEAN

Nurse writes letter dictated by Soldier 1.

Sweet little Bean,

Bean like the vegetable?

Sweet little Bean, I never got to see you but I know in my heart that you are beautiful.

I will always have with me the feel of the soft nudges on your mum's belly, and the joy I felt when we found out you were on the way.

I dream of you every night.

Don't you ever think that, since I wasn't around, that I didn't love you?

You were conceived of love and I came to this terrible place for love.

I am sorry. I did not want to have to write this letter.

There is so much I need to say, so much I need to share.

I hope some day you will understand why I never came home.

Please be proud of me, and don't let this stop you from loving life.

Look at the stars and know that I will be there with you, my sweet little Bean.

Your ever-loving father.

27 THE MIRACLE

Voiceover

I feel a breeze over my wet forehead. Where is everyone? I would love to eat something. But my jaws, they don't work. Or rub my tongue against my teeth. I can't. I haven't got a tongue, haven't got any teeth, my jaws are gone. Can't feel anything. All I have is this hole. If I had a mouth I would scream. Don't panic. Think. No eyes either. I can feel the wind touching my eyes but I don't see a thing. And my legs are so light. They've probably been cut off too. No wonder they feel light as air. Even a toenail is heavy compared to air. Never again to wiggle my toes. What a wonderful beautiful thing to wiggle your toes. I have nothing left. But I'm alive. I'm a miracle of modern science. This is no dream, I'm alive, for real! Pray for me. Pray for me.

28 *TELEPHONE* HARVEST MOON

Soldier 3 – *Mother*

Hello, Mother?

Hello, Son, how are you?

**We've just finished the dishes. I miss you.
Could you sing me a song?**

Which one would you like?

**The same song as ever. About the summer and the
autumn and the winter.**

> *SONG: Harvest Moon*
> Autumn comes,
> the summer is past,
> winter will come too soon.
> Stars will shine clearer,
> skies seem nearer
> under the Harvest Moon.
>
> Autumn comes,
> but let us be glad,
> singing an autumn tune.
> Hearts will be lighter,
> nights be brighter
> under the Harvest Moon.

**Wake me up Mother and tell me it's not real. Tell me I'm
not real.**

I don't know where you are, my son. But try to remember
that God is the only reality. And that you are made in his
image and lightness. And since you are the perfect reflection
of God's reality, you are real.

**No I'm not, Mother. Everything else is true but not this.
I remember the real things. What I am now is a dream.**

Nothing is less real about the waking dream of our mortal existence, than about the dream we have in sleep. Reality is God. And the essence of God is love. A perfect love which eradicates all fear and heals all wounds.

Stop it! I don't want to hear about God and love anymore.

29 NOT FOR ME

Voiceover

She is singing in the kitchen. I recognize the sound of the kitchen. She's singing to kill time.

Absent, while doing something else.

This war is not for me. This thing isn't any of my business. I don't care about making the world safe for democracy. All I want to do is live. I have no more to do with Germany, England or France than with the moon. Yet, here I am. Even though I couldn't care less. And I'm hurt, maybe worse than I think. I'm badly hurt, that much is certain. It might be better if I were dead and buried. Damn, why did I get into this mess? This isn't my fight. I never knew what this fight was all about.

30 THE FASCINATION

Nurse

War is simply a means to an end.

A rational, if very brutal, activity intended to serve the interests of one group of people. Whereby those who oppose that group are being killed or wounded.

Of course soldiers are not just machines out for gain or profit.

War exercises a powerful fascination and has a great impact on both participants and outsiders.

Fighting itself can be a source of joy. For some perhaps even the greatest joy of all.

Why else choose?

Voluntarily.

At the risk of dying.

To go into war.

To fight, to kill and be killed.

Soldier 1

I was curious. I wanted to be there, see it first-hand… But then they ask you to kill everything and everyone. And most of us actually do…

Nurse

In the Middle Ages people saw chivalry as God's highest command.

No empire, civilisation, nation, religion nor ideology has ever been able to blossom without excelling at war. Vigour is by far the strongest striking power.

Soldier 2

I believe in myself as part of war rather than in war as such. Everything is a matter of life and death. Nothing is boring. You live with all your senses heightened, alert. Your whole being concentrates on just one thing. All the rest is dispensable, erased.

You undergo an absolute feeling of a spiritual freedom most people will never know.

Nurse

I have no desire to experience that kind of freedom.

Soldier 2

Lots of people don't have the slightest idea that they also have a dark side. They wish they lived in a world where those emotions and lusts didn't exist. They just deny it. They don't realize war is like a natural disaster. Virtually unstoppable. The fact that one experiences so much beauty and pleasure in a situation that is supposed to be horrible, that's a conundrum for the Western mind.

Nurse

That is hell.

Soldier 3

If war were hell and only hell, I honestly don't think people would continue to wage war.

Nurse

How can the confrontation with death be a source of beauty?

Soldier 2

People fool themselves by explaining why they do what they do. But once you've conquered something, killed someone… There's something about it. Something ecstatic.

Very fulfilling. Horrible as well, to feel such a thing.
Obscene. It's rather pointless to deny it's very exciting.

Nurse

The act of killing isn't part of human nature, is it?

Soldier 3

My dog seems to find pleasure in the act of killing. It grabs
its prey, wounds it, plays with it and doesn't let go, and
when it's dead, it flaunts the body.

Soldier 2

Why should we be so different?

Nurse

Dogs?

Soldier 1

We are all curious about and fascinated by death.

Soldier 2

What if we are given power, even asked to slay simply by
moving a finger? Liquidating a human being. Power doesn't
get any stronger than this.

Nurse

For no reason, just out of the blue?

Soldier 2

Having a reason helps: feelings of revenge are easily
conjured up. It's probably the most powerful and least
controllable emotion. It provides instant satisfaction.

Soldier 3

Our group often quarrels over who exactly killed whom.
You want to take credit for your victims. But unless you're

a sniper, it's often hard to tell. So many bullets are whizzing around...

Nurse

For no reason?

Soldier 2

The real reason behind war has nothing to do with it. It is an individual struggle. Survival of the fittest.

Nurse

You express the horror so exquisitely.

Soldier 2

Even better: Ernst Jünger.

Soldier 1 playing Ernst Jünger

With his agile body, determined expression and bloodthirsty eyes he no longer feels any fatigue, pity or repentance, not even the pain of his own wounds.

A blind fury makes him ecstatic, overwhelms him with joy.

He experiences a kind of exalted, almost demoniacal lightness; which often goes hand in hand with fits of uncontrollable laughter.

In this condition, as if in a flash of lightning, he understands the true inner purpose and form of his life. He fights much harder than he could ever imagine.

Man is capable of greater things if he stops trying to distinguish cause from effect and gives in to the lighthearted game of life and death.

Nurse

They stop being self-contained individuals and become a part of something much bigger and more powerful than themselves; which indeed fills them with joy.

31 THE FULL UNIFORM

Voiceover

You're so numb that you go into battle quite serenely, without tears and without fear, yet we know full well that we are en route to sheer hell. In full uniform, however, your heart does not beat the way it wants. You're not yourself, you are barely a human being, at most a well-oiled automaton that performs without really thinking. My God, I do wish we could be human beings again!

32 TELEPHONE DEMOCRACY

Soldier 4 – *Father*

Dad, I need help. I'm in terrible trouble. Dad, can you hear me?

I hear you, Son, but I've got troubles of my own.

No, I mean serious trouble.

I can't help you. I have nothing to help you with. What would be of help to you? I have nothing myself.

You have me, don't you?

What's so special about you?

I may not be special now, but I'm going to be.

Of course you are. You're going to make the world safe for democracy's sake.

What is democracy?

Well I never got to the bottom of it myself. But I think it's got something to do with young men killing each other.

Why don't old men kill each other?

Well, the old men are needed to keep the home fires

burning.

Can't the young men do that just as well?

Young men don't have homes. That's why they have to go out and kill each other.

When my turn comes. Will you want me to go?

Any man would give his own son for democracy. I won't be here to stop you. Put your arms around me. I need your warmth.

That's impossible now, Father.

33 THE BEAST

Nurse

Our enemies are not the Germans, nor the Russians or the French. The common enemy of us all, is the beast within. Nowhere is this truth so clearly confirmed, as here, today.

Intoxicated, and excessively proud of our progress in science, of our culture and our state-of-the-art machines, 20th-century people had no other option but to admit that their civilization was as primitive as that of Attila the Hun. How infinitely sad to realize that two thousand years of Christianity went by without a trace of love thy neighbour.

34 ATILLA THE HUN

Soldier 2 playing Attila the Hun

Here you stand, after conquering mighty nations and subduing the world. I, Attila the Hun, therefore think it foolish for me to goad you with words, as though you were men who had not been proved in action.

For what is war but your usual custom?

What is sweeter than to seek revenge with your own hand?

You all know the Romans' cowardly habit of attacking civilians and killing any soul they could find without mercy for the weakest.

Aside from bodies of all ages you often find bodies of dogs chopped in two or severed legs of horses and cows' limbs.

They do this in an effort to scare the life out of us.

Let us attack this enemy vigorously and fast; they who attack are ever the bolder.

While they are forming their defense lines and hiding behind their ridiculous locked shields, they are already being checked by the dust of our fighting anger.

Let your courage rise and your own fury burst forth (the way we Huns do)!

No spear shall harm those who believe in their survival; those who fear death, however, Fate will overtake even in peace.

Why else would Fortune have made the Huns victorious over so many nations, if not to prepare them for the joy of this ultimate conflict.

This is the field so many victories promised us.

The enemy is close.

We are outnumbered, I know. So what? We are the rulers of Europe. For what reason would we now submit ourselves to the enemy?

Let us now talk with swords instead of words.

I shall hurl the first spear at the foe. If anyone can stand at rest while Attila fights, he is a dead man.

35 *SONG* RIDERS ON THE STORM

Into this house we're born
Into this world we're thrown…

36 THE ETERNAL SHORE

Nurse holds letter for Soldier 1 to read.

Soldier 1

Dear Willie,

This will be my last letter. The time has come to 'go over the top' and advance on the enemy trenches.

I'm quite ready, God was never nearer than he is now, even while the shells are bursting all around me. And I am trusting in Christ my Saviour to guide me to eternal light.

I may not always have given it my all, but I feel my sins are being forgiven through His love for me.

I am looking forward to this 'Great Push' to bring me a happy release from further military life, which I hate.

I hope to be wounded and sent home, or else be killed, either are preferable to this hell on earth.

I love you, dear, little brother. I shall think of you right to the end, and I shall pray to God to keep you in His Care.

I want you to be always good, spurn from your heart all evil and impure thoughts and fill your heart with Love for the Lord. Let no one ever tell you to go into war against any of your brothers or sisters. So will your soul stay pure and peaceful. War is a despicable means of settling affairs. I can do no better than this self-sacrifice which Jesus made.

We will meet again on the Eternal Shore.

Soldier 1 on his knees, praying.

Oh God, keep me from all harm in these dangerous hours. Bless my little brother with no mother or father. That he might live to become a brave and good man. And that we may meet bye-and-bye in Thy Presence. In the name of the Father, the Son and the Holy Spirit.

Soldier 1 goes into shell-shock.

37 THE SYNDROME

Nurse – Soldier1

The Greeks referred to this as 'war nostalgia' because homesickness caused the symptoms among young soldiers.

Since Napoleon it has been called 'war trauma'.

Mr Freud says it is a neurotic dysfunction caused by the unconscious suppressing of fear.

The General calls them parasites and impostors and sends them back into battle.

On November 7th 1918 a deserter with those symptoms is to be executed by his own platoon for the very last time.

The doctor talks about 'shell-shock'. According to him it's the result of the displacement of air caused by exploding bombs. The so-called shell blast.

During the Second World War it will be called 'combat fatigue'.

And later on: PTSS. Post Traumatic Stress Syndrome.

You can get it when you survive a certain life-threatening situation. A situation where you expect to die. But you don't.

This causes several reactions in the brain, which are translated into 14-odd symptoms. Of course you don't need to show all 14. But a high level of irritation, flashbacks, uncontrollable spasms, nightmares, acute anxiety, explosions of anger and depression are the most common.

You know how women behave, how they latch on to men. Especially when those men are in uniform. Then...

And, of course: the more symptoms, the more serious the condition.

Have you ever watched the girls when a regiment passes through their village? They're all over the place. The soldiers don't have to lift a finger. They're an easy prey. The men are not to blame for the fact that most women in war zones are totally degenerated.

I am no longer a woman. Haven't been for ages. There are no men here. What you'll find here are mangled testicles, chests with holes in, stumps where there used to be limbs, noseless or jawless faces. But no men. So how on earth could I be a woman?

In occupied territory things are different, of course. Behind enemy lines, the occupying army forces itself upon the women, violently. Savages! Then you're better off being ugly as hell, or old, or retarded. If not...you're a sitting duck. Of course, after the war, no decent man will want to mate with those women. That door's closed forever.

I can plump up a pillow. Bring cups of cold water to lips, put a needle inside a cramped body. But I can never chase away the horror. That bedside devil always wins.

You're useless, aren't you?

You really don't have the first clue.

I should kill you.

Why's that?

To exterminate you from society.

Is that so?

You bet.

People like you should be destroyed.

They disturb life.

Aren't you the one disturbing life?

Shut up! I provide arguments. I will prove my point.

I get up early.

I work myself to the bone...

Why, why do you have to get up so early? You're missing the point.

Why would you want to kill me?

Because you don't understand the goal of life.

My heart is dead.
I killed it myself.
I hated to feel it dance inside my chest,
while this terribly sick animal is suffocating in my arms.

Then you have to live by the rules, by the script.

I have toughened up.

I'm efficient now.

Suitable for handling Gods and Demons.

A machine with barely any trace of a woman inside.

Vapid, past salvation.

Sometimes a pillow beams a flicker of a smile at me, and I die inside.

It is impossible to be a woman in here.

That's for sure, bitch.

Whore, cunt, get off! stupid...

Nurse leaves in tears.

38 A DREAM

Voiceover

I'm nothing. I'm just a piece of meat that keeps on living. Since my real life is a bigger nightmare than my dreams, it would be cruel to pretend anyone can help me. I can only hope for a miracle. No, not a miracle. Maybe it would be better to pretend I am a dream. Never been something else. A dream like all dreams that never comes true. I don't know whether or not I'm alive and dreaming or dead and remembering. Am I getting older? Will anyone ever come to visit me? I hope not. I wouldn't want anyone to see me like this.

39 *TELEPHONE* CAN'T TALK

Soldier 4 – *Sweetie*

Hello?

Why didn't you write?

I couldn't write. I just couldn't.

Why not?

I can't tell you. I just can't.

You don't love me.

I do love you. Really, I do.

You need help.

There isn't any help for me.

Maybe ask for some.

I can't ask anything, I can't talk.

Then why don't you send a telegram?

A telegram?

Use your head, will you? Think.

Yes, my head, my head, hello? She's gone.

40 *SONG* SILENT NIGHT

Silent night, holy night
All is calm, all is bright
Round yon Virgin Mother and Child
Holy Infant so tender and mild
Sleep in heavenly peace
Sleep in heavenly peace.

41 NOT EVEN GOD

Voiceover

I will never get out of here. They'll never let me go. They'll keep me here as a secret. Till I'm old and worn out. Then I'll sneak out of here and die. It isn't easy, though. Inside me I'm screaming and yelling and howling like a trapped animal. But nobody pays any attention. If I had arms I could kill myself. If I had legs I could run away. If I had a voice, I could talk and be some kind of company to myself. I could yell for help. But nobody would help me. Not even God, 'cause there isn't any God. Couldn't be in a place like this. And yet, I've got to do something. But I don't know how. Help me, help me, help me.

THE END

WWW.OBERONBOOKS.COM